Responsib

by Kelli L. Hicks

Content Consultants:
Melissa Z. Pierce, L.C.S.W.
Sam Williams, M.Ed.

Rourke
Educational Media

rourkeeducationalmedia.com

Teacher Notes available at
rem4teachers.com

www.rourkeeducationalmedia.com

Melissa Z. Pierce is a licensed clinical social worker with a background in counseling in the home and school group settings. Melissa is currently a life coach. She brings her experience as a L.C.S.W. and parent to the *Little World Social Skills* collection and the *Social Skills and More* program.

Sam Williams has a master's degree in education. Sam is a former teacher with over ten years of classroom experience. He has been a literacy coach, professional development writer and trainer, and is a published author. He brings his experience in child development and classroom management to this series.

PHOTO CREDITS: Cover: © Kai Chiang; Page 3: © kali9; Page 5: © Anke Van Wyk; Page 6: © Craig Dingle; Page 7: © Sean Locke; Page 9: © Troels Graugaard; Page 11: © Agnieszka Kirinicjanow; Page 13: © Brian Toro; Page 15: © PenelopeB; Page 17: © kristian sekulic; Page 19: © jianying yin
Illustrations by: Anita DuFalla

Edited by: Precious McKenzie

Cover and Interior designed by: Tara Raymo

Library of Congress PCN Data

Responsibility / Kelli L. Hicks
(Little World Social Skills)
ISBN 978-1-61810-130-3 (hard cover)(alk. paper)
ISBN 978-1-61810-263-8 (soft cover)
Library of Congress Control Number: 2011945274

Rourke Educational Media
Printed in the United States of America,
North Mankato, Minnesota

rourkeeducationalmedia.com

customerservice@rourkeeducationalmedia.com • PO Box 643328 Vero Beach, Florida 32964

Do you know what it means to be responsible?

If you make good choices and help at **school** and at home you are showing responsibility.

When you take out the
garbage or set the table for
dinner, it helps your family.

How do you show responsibility?

Your school probably has **rules** to keep you safe. When you follow the rules, even if others don't, you are showing responsibility.

Do you **recycle**? When you recycle plastic or paper, you are showing responsibility for keeping our planet clean.

Being responsible can be hard. Sometimes you might want to watch TV when it is your turn to help with the **dishes.**

What would a responsible person do?

When you show responsibility, you help even if you would rather be doing something else.

When you show responsibility, others will notice. You might get to be your teacher's helper.

It feels good to be responsible and it makes others **proud** of you, too!

How can you show responsibility?

Picture Glossary

dishes (DISH-ez):
Containers you have at home such as plates or bowls.

garbage (GAR-bij):
The things you no longer want or need.

proud (proud):
The feeling you have when you feel good about your actions.

recycle (ree-SYE-kuhl):
When we reuse paper, plastic, metal, and glass to make new products.

rules (ROOLZ):
The instructions that tell you what you can and cannot do.

school (SKOOL):
A place where people go to learn.

Index

Websites

www.scholastic.com/teachers/lesson-plan/
   teacher-made-activities-teaching-responsibility

www.play-activities.com/blog/
   teaching-young-children-responsibility/

www.kids.gov/k_5/k_5_fun_activities.shtml

About the Author

Kelli L. Hicks lives in Tampa where she is responsible for her husband, two children, Mackenzie and Barrett, and taking her dog Gingerbread for walks (even when she is too tired).

Ask The Author!
www.rem4students.com

24